Iina-Marja's Day

To the Juuso family – Iina-Marja, Sara-Inga, Aslak-Johan and Per-Oula

Iina-Marja's Day copyright © Frances Lincoln Limited 2002
Text and photographs copyright © Jaakko Alatalo 2002
The Publishers would like to acknowledge Prodeepta Das as the originator of the series of which this book forms a part.
Prodeepta Das is the author and photographer of *Geeta's Day*.

First published in Great Britain in 2002 by Frances Lincoln Limited,
4 Torriano Mews, Torriano Avenue, London NW5 2RZ

First paperback published in Great Britain in 2009

British Cataloguing in Publication Data available on request

ISBN 978-1-84507-993-2

Printed in Singapore

1 3 5 7 9 8 6 4 2

AUTHOR ACKNOWLEDGEMENTS
With grateful thanks to Iina-Marja and her family. Thanks also to Iina-Marja's teacher Taina Syväjärvi,
all the staff and pupils at Karesuvanto school and to Iina-Marja's best-friend Berit-Anne;
to Helena and Nils-Henrik Valkeapää for advising me on Sami language and culture; to the pilot Risto Anunti;
to Eero Haapala for making all the necessary contacts; and to my wife Anja for the support she has given me throughout.

Iina-Marja's Day

From Dawn to Dusk in Lapland

Jaakko Alatalo

F

FRANCES LINCOLN
CHILDREN'S BOOKS

AUTHOR'S NOTE

Iina-Marja and her family live in *Sápmi* (Samiland), in a region of Northern Europe called Lapland. Lapland covers a wide area and includes parts of northern Norway, Sweden, Finland and Russia. Iina-Marja's village lies near the river Muonionjoki, which is the border between Finland and Sweden. The Finnish side of the village, where Iina-Marja lives, is called Karesuvanto, and the Swedish side, across the river, is called Karesuando.

Lapland takes its name from the Lapp people who first lived there thousands of years ago. These days the Lapp people prefer to be known as 'Sami' people, because this is what they call themselves in their own language. Iina-Marja and her family are amongst the 6,000 or so Sami people living in Finland (most people who live in Finland today are Finnish). They usually stay in Karesuvanto during the week, but they spend their weekends and the summer at their second home in Raittijärvi, in the Arctic wilderness. At Raittijärvi they tend their reindeer herd, go fishing and hunting, and spend time together around the fire in the *goahti* (a cone-shaped tent).

Iina-Marja Juuso is seven years old.

She lives in a village in Finnish Lapland with her mother Sara-Inga and her father Aslak-Johan. Iina-Marja's older brother, Per-Oula, looks after the family's reindeer herd at their second home in Raittijärvi.

Iina-Marja and her family are wearing the traditional dress of the Sami people. It is made from fine wool, and keeps them warm even when it gets wet. Nowadays, only older Sami people wear traditional dress every day, but Sami children like to wear it on special occasions.

1

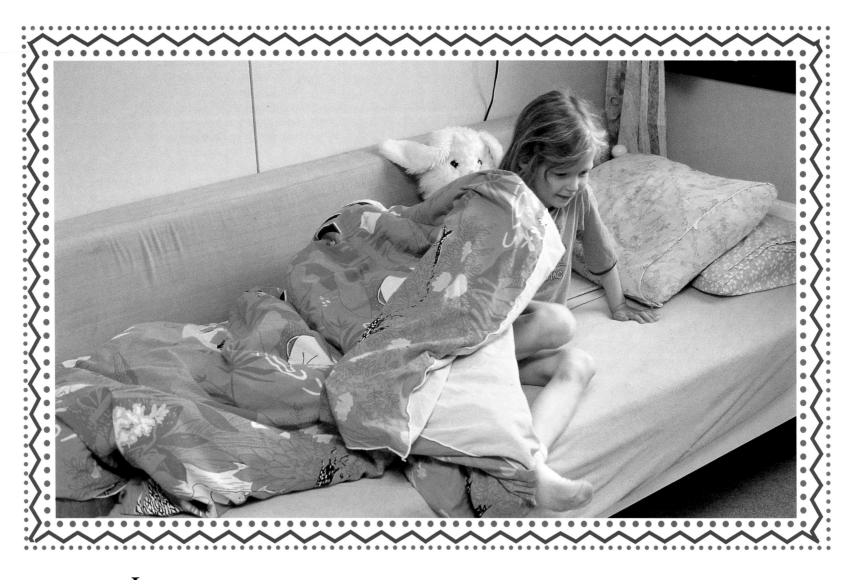

Iina-Marja gets up at seven o'clock. The house is always very quiet at this time of the morning. All Iina-Marja can hear is a couple of magpies squawking outside in the garden. She thinks they must be teasing her dog Musti because he soon starts barking.

The first thing Iina-Marja does when she's up is go to the bathroom to brush her teeth and wash her face.

Next she brushes her hair. She has plenty of time as she never has any breakfast. She prefers just to drink a glass of orange juice.

Iina-Marja's best-friends, Berit-Anne and Ellen-Marit, live a few doors away. Today it is their mother's turn to drive them all to school. At about eight o'clock, Iina-Marja says goodbye to her mother and gets into the car with her friends.

Before they go in for lessons this morning, the children play an exciting game of *Noaidi* (Witch).

NOAIDI The child who is the Noaidi has to catch the other children and put them in prison under one of the school's trees. Another tree has been chosen as a safe place where the Noaidi cannot go. The children who are free have to run from the safe tree past the Noaidi to try to save the prisoners.

There are only four Sami pupils at Karesuvanto school, and Iina-Marja is one of them. The other 42 pupils are Finnish. The Sami children are taught separately so that they can have lessons in their own Sami language. They start the day by singing a hymn called 'God Created the Flowers'.

The first lesson is writing. Iina-Marja has excellent handwriting for her age. Because she is left-handed, the teacher has to write out the exercises specially for her on the right-hand side of the page. Otherwise she would cover them up with her writing hand.

The teacher asks Iina-Marja to write the word 'Sápmelaš' on the board, which is the word for a Sami person in Sami language. In Finnish, it is 'Saamelainen'. Like her three classmates, Iina-Marja can speak both Sami and Finnish very well.

In the break between lessons, Iina-Marja has a go on the *suhkan* (swing). She makes the suhkan go so high, she wonders if it will take her all the way over the top of the bar and round again!

After break, they carry on with their lessons. Jon-Isak has to finish his spelling exercises before he can play the word game on the floor with the girls.

Later on in the morning, one of teachers takes them for a walk. They have fun playing Follow My Leader up and down the little hills of earth in the school grounds, which the builders made recently when doing some repairs. All the exercise makes Iina-Marja feel hungry.

After their lunch of chicken and rice, school is over for the day as there are only morning lessons on Friday. Iina-Marja's mother picks her up and they go shopping in Sweden, which is on the other side of the Muonionjoki river. They buy bread, margarine and some *eppeliid* (apples).

EPPELIID *Lapland is too cold to grow eppeliid so they are brought in from countries with warmer climates, like Germany, France and Denmark.*

10

As soon as they get home, Iina-Marja runs round to their nearest neighbour, her *áhkku* (grandmother). They go outside together to the *goahti* (tent) in her garden.

GOAHTI A long time ago, when the Sami people wandered with their reindeer herds between summer and winter pastures, the goahti was their only home. They carried everything they needed on the back of their reindeer sledges and put up their goahti whenever they wanted to rest. They made it warm and cosy inside by lighting a fire and covering the ground with reindeer pelts (skins).

When they are settled inside, Iina-Marja tells áhkku all about her morning at school. Áhkku has an ordinary house, too, but she and Iina-Marja prefer spending time around the fire in the goahti.

Iina-Marja can't stay long with áhkku, because her mother has promised to give her a sewing lesson. They are making a *sisteseahkka* (leather pouch) out of reindeer leather.

By learning to make things with reindeer leather, Iina-Marja is carrying on a Sami tradition. Sami people have always made good use of their reindeer – they eat reindeer meat, they make clothes, shoes and bags from reindeer skins, and they carve beautiful knives and spoons out of reindeer bone.

Before she and her mother leave to go to their other home for the weekend, Iina-Marja and her friend Berit-Anne play a game of Catch the Reindeer. Berit-Anne holds a pair of antlers and pretends to be a reindeer and Iina-Marja swings her rope until she manages to hook it around the antlers. "Got you!" shouts Iina-Marja, when she catches Berit-Anne at last.

Then it's time to make the journey to Raittijärvi, where Iina-Marja's father and brother have been working all week. There are no roads to Raittijärvi so they travel by seaplane. Iina-Marja's father meets them at the jetty in the buggy.

RAITTIJÄRVI is a reindeer-tending village in the Arctic wilderness. The reindeer are kept in large enclosures and graze on lichen (a type of fungus that grows on tree trunks and on the ground), mushrooms and grass.

15

They are having reindeer for dinner this evening so, when they have unpacked their things, Iina-Marja's father cuts up some reindeer meat.

They take the meat into the kitchen for cooking. Sara-Inga is going to boil it in a big saucepan with some salt.

While they eat their dinner of reindeer, *buđehat* (potatoes) and *rohkaláibi* (rye bread), they talk about the things that have happened in the week. Iina-Marja's father and her brother Per-Oula have been working hard, repairing holes in the fences around the enclosures.

After dinner, Iina-Marja prepares the boat and they go fishing. Soon winter will come and the lake will freeze over. It will stay frozen for about eight months, until mid-summer. When the lake is frozen, Iina-Marja has to make a hole in the ice before she can lower her fishing net into the water.

It is Iina-Marja's job to clean the *čuovža* (whitefish). First she removes the scales of the čuovža by scraping the sides with a knife. Then she cuts them open and removes all the bits from the inside. Finally, she cleans the čuovža in fresh cold water. Now they are ready for her mother to cook for lunch tomorrow.

Then Iina-Marja helps her father take some wood into the house for the fire. Their home in Raittijärvi is new, and this wood is left over from when they built it. When it runs out, Per-Oula will cut down some birch trees to use instead.

It is almost bedtime. Before Iina-Marja goes in for the night, she sits in the goahti with her father while he smokes some reindeer meat.

Smoking meat gives it a good flavour, but more importantly it means that it will stay fresh throughout the long winter ahead. In the past, people in the wilderness did not have freezers, so smoking meat was the only way to conserve it.

Iina-Marja is very tired by the time she gets into her bed. She looks at her *Vulle Vuojaš* (Donald Duck) cartoon book for while, but she soon falls fast asleep. Tomorrow her father will take her to see the reindeer. *Buorre ija, Iina-Marja.* (Good night, Iina-Marja.)

MORE ABOUT LAPLAND AND FINLAND

Lapland spreads across the northern parts of Norway, Sweden, Finland and Russia. The part of Lapland that is in Finland – called Finnish Lapland – takes up almost half of Finland. Although many people like to visit Finnish Lapland to see the reindeer and go skiing and hill walking, not many people live there all the time because the land is so wild and barren.

Most of Lapland is above the Arctic Circle. The Arctic Circle is the imaginary line that geographers have drawn around the northern part of the world (ask someone to show it to you on a globe). Lapland's position means that the sun does not set in summer – so there is continuous light for about two months – and does not rise in the winter months – so there is continuous darkness. The long, dark Lappish winter is called *skábma* in Sami language.

When people look at the sky in Lapland, they are treated to a beautiful sight – the northern lights (or 'aurora borealis', as they are sometimes called). The northern lights are like greeny-white curtains that swirl across the sky. The ancient Laplanders believed they were caused by a giant fox swishing his tail near the North Pole.

THE PAST

The very first people to live in Finland, about 6,000 years ago, were the Sami people. When the Finnish people arrived about 2,000 years later they overpowered the Sami tribes and forced them to flee to the north of the country, to Lapland.

The Finnish tribes fought amongst themselves and made money from selling fur to the neighbouring countries until, in the middle ages, the powerful Swedes claimed Finland for themselves. The Swedes ruled Finland for hundreds of years (which is why there are so many Swedish-speaking people in Finland today). But eventually, while the Swedish king was away somewhere else in the Swedish empire, the Russians invaded and Finland became part of the Russian empire instead.

After a war with Russia, Finland finally became an independent country in 1917. The Russians tried very hard to get Finland back during the Second World War, but they were not successful.

RELIGION

Most Sami people today, like most people in Finland, are Christians. But in ancient times the Sami had their own religion, which developed out of their close relationship with nature. They believed in many gods and called upon them for help when they were out hunting or when they were hungry or ill.

The Sami also believed there was an underworld, where all sorts of gnomes and trolls lived. The most frightening creature of all in the Sami underworld was a giant called *Stállu*. When Iina-Marja's grandmother was a girl, her mother used to say that if she was naughty, Stállu would come out of the forest and take her away in a big sack!

THE PEOPLE

It is said in Lapland that Sami people never get lost in the wilderness. This is because they are so used to living close to nature. Even if it is freezing cold and there is a snowstorm, the Sami reindeer owners have to get on with their work outside, tending to their herd. No one worries much about the time out in the Arctic wilderness. Sami people follow nature's clock: they eat when they are hungry and sleep when they are tired. But not all Sami people follow the traditional Sami way of life. It can be hard to find jobs in Lapland so some young Sami people move to other parts of Finland in order to study and work.

LANGUAGE IN LAPLAND AND FINLAND

There are nine different Sami languages altogether, but only three of these – Northern Sami, Inari Sami and Scolt Sami – are spoken in Finland. The other six are spoken in other areas of Lapland, in Sweden, Norway and Russia. The most widely spoken Sami language in Finland is Northern Sami. This is the version of Sami which Iina-Marja speaks, and which is used in her schoolbooks and on Sami radio.

Because of the different peoples that live there, Finland has three official languages: Finnish, Swedish and Sami. They are called 'official' languages because people are entitled by law to use them in the official, public areas of their lives. This means that if a Sami person goes to their local post-office, library, hospital or law court in Finnish Lapland, they have the right to be talked to in their own Sami language – even though there are only about 2,000 regular Sami speakers in the whole of Finland. Most people in Finland, including most Sami people, speak Finnish.

Languages can tell you a lot about the people who speak them. One interesting thing about Sami language is that there are over twenty words for reindeer. *Vuobirs* means a two-year-old male reindeer, for example, and *áldu* is a two-year-old female reindeer that has a calf.

SOME SAMI WORDS AND PHRASES

buorre beaivi – hello
Mii du namma lea? –
   What is your name?
Mu namma lea Iina-Marja –
   My name is Iina-Marja
Mo veaját? – How are you?
Mun ealán dearvan – I am fine
giittus eatnat – thank you very much
báze dearvan – goodbye

THE SAMI AND FINNISH WORDS IN THE BOOK

áhkku – grandma

buđehat – potatoes

Buorre ija, Iina-Marja – Good night, Iina-Marja

čuovža – whitefish. Čuovža are very common in the deep, cold lakes of Lapland. They have large silvery scales and small heads. People sometimes smoke čuovža to conserve it, in the same way that they smoke reindeer meat

eppeliid – apples

goahti – the traditional dwelling of the Sami people. The ancient Sami made their goahti from the materials they found around them in the wilderness. They constructed the cone-shaped frame from lengths of birchwood (the wood that Iina-Marja's family use for fuel at Raittijärvi) and then placed reindeer skins over the top and on the ground inside so that they would stay warm and dry

Muonionjoki – the river that flows between Finland and Sweden

Noaidi – Witch, a game that Iina-Marja and her friends play at school. In ancient times, before the Christian missionaries arrived in Lapland and converted the Sami to Christianity, the noaidi acted as the messenger between the people and the Sami gods

rohkaláibi – bread made from rye flour

Saamelainen – the word for a Sami person in Finnish

Sápmelaš – the word for a Sami person in Sami language

Sápmi – Samiland, the area in Lapland where most of the Sami people live

sisteseahkka – a pouch made from reindeer leather

skábma – the Sami word for the long, cold Arctic winter, when the sun never rises and it is always dark outside

Stállu – a character in old Sami religion

suhkan – swing

Vulle Vuojaš – Donald Duck

INDEX